This book belongs to:

_____

*Sesame Subjects* is a series of first nonfiction books for little kids that are filled with just the sort of fascinating and fun facts that children love learning.

Chock-full of colorful and engaging photos and eye-catching diagrams and drawings, each book covers a single subject and offers just the right amount of information for a child to take in, sparking further curiosity and learning. *Sesame Subjects* will feed a child's sense of discovery and wonder at the ever-expanding world around her.

Published by Creative Edge, 2010, an imprint of Dalmatian Publishing Group, Franklin, Tennessee 37067. No part of this book may be reproduced or copied in any form without written permission from the copyright owner. 1-800-815-8696

Printed in the U.S.A

CE12308/0210/NGS

## My First Book About
# THE FIVE SENSES

By Kama Einhorn

Illustrated by Christopher Moroney

Creative Edge

**H**ello, everybodee! It is I, Professor Grover, and Elmo. Today we are here to learn all about the five senses.

Inside this cute furry head of Elmo's is a BRAIN. Without my brain, I would not be Grover. Without his brain, Elmo would not be Elmo. Without your brain, you would not be you. You get the general idea.

Your brain does amazing things. It lets you see, hear, taste, smell, and feel. You are using your brain right now to read this book. Now please put your hand on your head. Give your brain inside a little pat. Very good.

Are you ready to put on your thinking cap? Very good.

see

hear

taste

smell

feel

# Every person has a brain inside his or her skull.

One more time, knock very gently on your head. The hard part you feel is your skull.

Your skull protects your brain. You can help take care of your brain by eating healthy foods, getting regular sleep, and always wearing a helmet to protect it when riding a bike, rollerskating, and playing other sports.

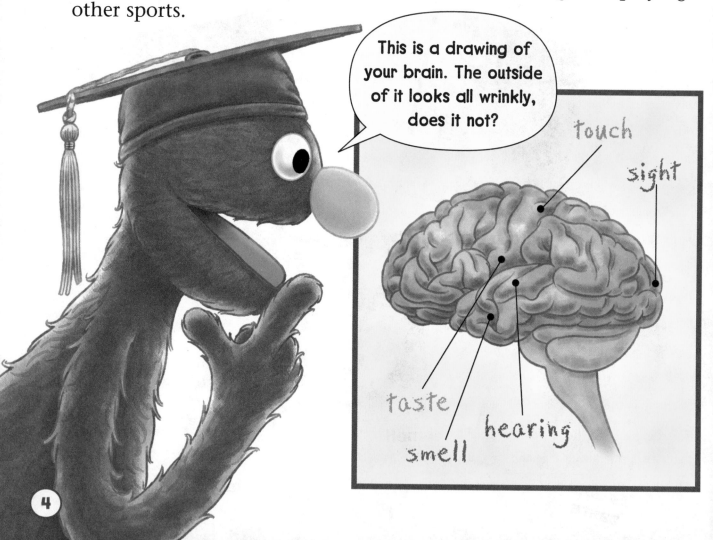

This is a drawing of your brain. The outside of it looks all wrinkly, does it not?

touch

sight

taste

smell

hearing

# Different parts of your brain let you . . .

These are some of the things that Elmo's brain lets Elmo do.

**think**

**remember**

**talk**

**move**

**feel emotions**

I will give you a hint about what is happening on the next page. The clues are these different parts of your body. Think hard.

# Your brain is like the boss of your whole body.

It lets you see, hear, taste, smell, and feel.

These things are called your senses. You have five of them.

> See? The five senses. Count them. FIVE.

You use your eyes to see.

You use your ears to hear.

**You use your tongue to taste.**

**You use your nose to smell.**

**You use your hands to feel.**

But eyes, ears, tongues, noses, and skin cannot do their jobs all by themselves. Your brain helps these parts of your body tell you what is going on. Your brain tells you what your eyes see, what your ears hear, what your tongue tastes, what your nose smells, and what your skin feels. The skin on your hands is some of the most sensitive skin on your body.

# Seeing

You use your eyes to see.

The pupil is an opening in your eye. When you see something—a tree, for example—light comes in through your pupils.

The light helps make a picture inside your eye of what you are looking at.

The picture travels to your brain, and then your brain tells you that you are seeing a tree.

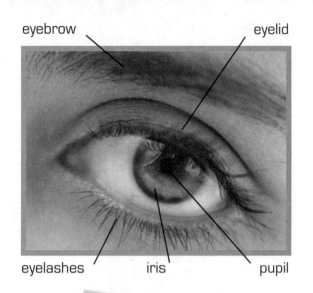

eyebrow

eyelid

eyelashes

iris

pupil

Eyebrows, eyelids, and eyelashes all help protect your eyes from dirt and dust.

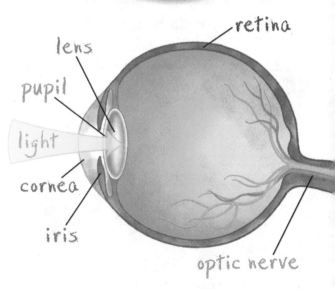

lens

retina

pupil

light

cornea

iris

optic nerve

An eye doctor checks your vision. Some people need glasses to help them see better.

Pupils change size depending on how much light they need to let into your eyes.

The colored part of your eye is called the iris. What color are your irises?

A magnifying glass is a lens that makes things look bigger.

# Hearing

You use your ears to hear.

When something moves, the air around it moves. The moving air creates sound waves. The sound waves are then picked up by your ears.

Finally, your brain gets a message from your ears that you have heard a sound.

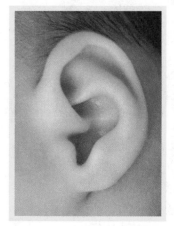

**outer ear** auricle

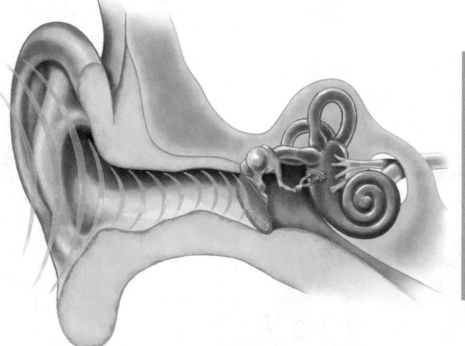

Cupping your hand to your ear helps capture sound. You try it!

Your outer ear is made of cartilage. It feels a little bit like soft bone or maybe even rubber. But most of your ear is actually *inside* your head!

Some sounds are nice to hear.

music

Some are **NOT**!

Honk! Honk!

traffic

Animals like foxes and rabbits hear very well because their ears can move to catch sound.

The smallest bone in your whole body is in your ear. It is smaller than a grain of rice! It is called the stirrup.

I like to listen to myself sing. Do I not sound wonderful?

La la la!

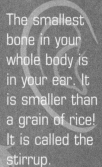

stirrup

11

# Tasting

You use your tongue to taste. It helps you know what flavor your food or drink is.

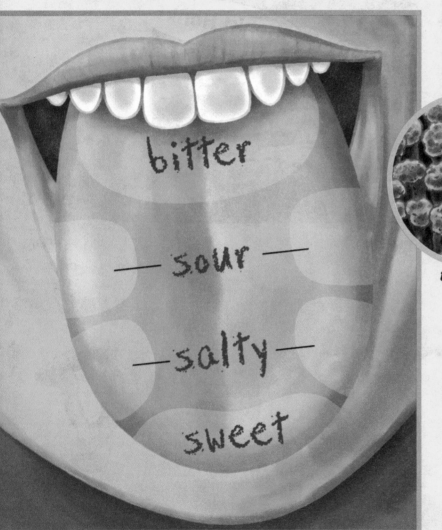

bitter

— sour —

—salty—

sweet

taste buds

You have about 10,000 tiny bumps called taste buds in your mouth. Most of them are on your tongue. The taste buds on different parts of your tongue let you taste different things. The taste buds tell your brain what you are tasting.

**bitter greens**

**sour lemon**

**sweet cake**

**salty pretzel**

Hello! Me come to visit. Me expert on taste. Me love sweet taste of COOKIES!

# Smelling

You use your nose to smell. Your sense of smell also helps you to taste things.

The nose knows. Get it? The nose knows how to smell a rose! And my toes! And whatever the wind blows! Oh, I am so funny.

Just about everything has a smell. But you cannot see smells.

Does this boy look like he likes what he is smelling?

Garlic has a strong scent.

**GROVER'S HOMEWORK**

Smell something like a flower. Now take a really BIG sniff of the same thing. Can you tell the difference? When you sniffed really hard, more of the smell reached higher inside your nose, so it smelled stronger.

Have you ever smelled the strong odor of a skunk? It is very stinky! Skunks spray their stinky scent when they want another animal—including people— to leave them alone. It works!

# Feeling/Touching

You use your skin to feel touch. Your fingers are especially sensitive— which means they are good at feeling.

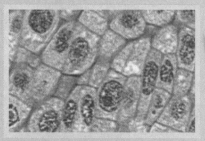

magnified skin cells

Your whole body is covered with skin. Your skin is very sensitive.

With my sense of touch, I can feel how SOFT and FURRY Elmo is.

Look closely at your fingertips. Do you see your fingerprints? Everyone's fingerprints are different.

Your skin can feel if something is hot or cold, smooth or rough. It can send a message to your brain to let you know whether something hurts or feels good.

**smooth**

**rough**

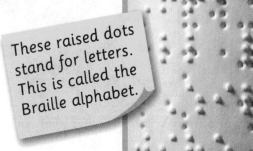

When one of your senses does not work, the other four senses work harder. People who cannot see can use their sense of touch to read!

These raised dots stand for letters. This is called the Braille alphabet.

**Braille**

We have used our brains so much—to learn ABOUT our brains! So, now I, Grover, would like to invite you to my five-senses party!

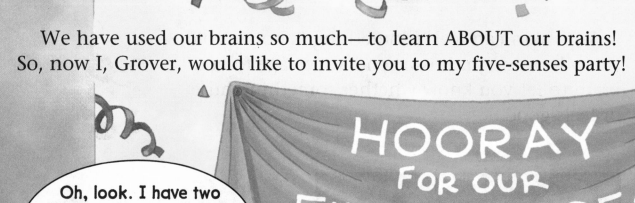

HOORAY FOR OUR FIVE SENSES

Oh, look. I have two good friends at this party. I SEE that one is blue and one is red.

Cookie Monster made some cookies. They SMELL so yummy baking in the oven!

These cookies TASTE sooo good.

Mmm, this glass of milk FEELS so nice and cold in my hand. And cold milk goes so well with warm cookies.

My five senses are sending all sorts of messages to my brain about what is going on at this party. I, Grover, am seeing, hearing, tasting, smelling, and feeling! And it's all happening right here—in my wonderful brain!

And Elmo can HEAR from all the munching and crunching that Cookie Monster is enjoying the cookies, too!

Crunch! Crunch!

# "EXTRA-CREDIT" FUN FOR EVERYONE!

If you want to know more about your five senses, here are some fun things you can do with your family.

### SEEING

Gather paint chips (color samples) from a paint store. Sort them into different piles. How many different shades of each color are there? You can glue the colors onto a large piece of paper to make a rainbow. Use a different color group for each band in the rainbow. You can also do this with crayons or colored pencils.

### HEARING

Play a hearing guessing game. Have a grown-up close his or her eyes and try to guess what sound you are making. Tap spoons on a table, shake dry rice in a container, jingle coins in your hand, crumple up some paper or foil, close a book, bounce a ball. Then switch places.

### TASTING

Gather small pieces of food with different flavors: a pretzel (salty), a slice of lemon (sour), a sugar cube (sweet), a small piece of orange peel (bitter). Touch the food to different areas of your tongue (look at page 12 for the "taste map" of your tongue). Does it taste stronger in different places? Now try each one again with your nose plugged! How does that affect the taste?

## SMELLING

Gather six small plastic containers. Get some cinnamon, vinegar, coffee grounds, onion, ginger, and so on. Put one thing in each container, close your eyes, and smell. Try to guess what is in each container. Are the smells strong or weak? Which ones do you like? Which ones do not smell good to you?

## FEELING/TOUCHING

Ask an adult to wrap one of your hands loosely in a plastic bag. Leave the other unwrapped. Touch something with the bagged hand, then touch it with the bare one. How does it feel different?

See you later. With our eyes, of course!

Bye-bye.